C000139942

Happy Christmas!

I got my wife a wooden le̶
It's not her main present, ̶

The MP Thomas Massey-Massey proposed a motion to change the name of Christmas to "Christ-tide" (on the grounds that mass is Catholic; the UK Protestant): "He was interrupted by a member opposite who asked him how he would like to be called 'Thotide Tidey-Tidey'. The bill was forgotten in the uproar."

There's nothing sadder in this world than to awake Christmas morning and not be a child.

I always spell plumb-pudding (so) – I think it sounds fatter and more suetty.

LAMB, LETTERS

'What's Christmas time to you but a time for paying bills without money; a time for finding yourself a year older, but not an hour richer? ... If I could work my will,' said Scrooge indignantly, 'every idiot who goes about with "Merry Christmas" on his lips, should be boiled with his own pudding, and buried with a stake of holly through his heart.'

CHARLES DICKENS

You can tell a lot about a person by the way s/he handles three things: a rainy day, lost luggage and tangled Christmas tree lights.

MAYA ANGELOU

I find the sentiments of Barbara Ehrenreich refreshing. This is from her book Natural Causes, Life, Death and the Illusion of Control.

In the last few years I have given up on the many medical measures – cancer screenings, annual exams, Pap smears, for example – expected of a responsible person with health insurance. This was not based on any suicidal impulse. It was barely even a decision, more like an accumulation of micro-decisions: to stay at my desk and meet a deadline or show up at the primary care office and submit to the latest test to gauge my biological sustainability; to spend the afternoon in the faux-cosy corporate environment of a medical facility or go for a walk…

At first I criticised myself as a slacker and procrastinator, falling behind on the simple, obvious stuff that could prolong my life. After all, this is the great promise of modern scientific medicine: You do not have to get sick and die (at least not for a while), because problems can be detected 'early' when they are readily treatable. Better to catch a tumour, when it's the size of an olive than that of a canteloupe…

I had a different reaction to aging: I gradually came to realise that I was old enough to die…

Once I realised that I was old enough to die, I decided that I was also old enough not to incur any more suffering, annoyance, or boredom in the pursuit of a longer life. I eat well, meaning I choose foods that taste good, and that will stave off hunger for as long as possible, like protein, fibre and fats. I exercise, not because it will make me live longer, but because it feels good when I do. As for medical care: I will seek help for an urgent problem, but I am no longer interested in looking for problems that remain undetectable to me. Ideally, the determination of when one is old enough to die should be a personal decision, based on a judgement of the likely benefits, if any, of medical care and – just as important at a certain age – how we choose to spend the time that remains to us.

The 'crabbed and humorous Oxonian', Geoffrey Madan, had an eye for aphorisms, and each Christmas between 1929 and 1933 he sent a small anthology to his friends. A selection was collected in 1981 and published as Geoffrey Madan's Notebooks.

Churchgoers, and 'good' people generally, do just what ordinary decent people do about anything: only they do it slower.

A C BENSON

Safe remarks:

1. To an inaudible remark: "That's just what I've been wondering all the evening."
2. "I can never remember how you spell your name." (But G.M. Young quoted the man who wearily replied, "Still J-O-N-E-S.")

Alive, in the sense that he can't be legally buried.

Of all tyrannies a country can suffer, the worst is the tyranny of the majority.

DEAN INGE

Madam, the Wings of Opportunity are Fledged with the Feathers of Death.

DRAKE, TO ELIZABETH

"My dear, you're the only woman in the world who'd have known the right hat to wear on an occasion like this."

OSCAR WILDE, TO MRS LEVERSON, ON HIS COMING OUT OF PRISON

Nile Rodgers is a songwriter. I read his biography Le Freak *this year and I was intrigued by how he tried to inject 'Deep Hidden Meaning' into his lyrics.*

I often say that every single song I've ever written is non-fiction, with fictional elements. So there's an essential truth, but you need these other colours to paint in, to fill in the blanks, because the core truth is in fact stable, and what it is, the colours are to make it clearer and easier to understand. The stuff that seems to touch us the best, is when it's a mixture of both those worlds.

Artists are storytellers, they're not just egotistical people that want to pump themselves up. They're people that want to share their knowledge and information and opinions about the things that they see. When I was a very young teen music student, my teacher told me that once, any time, any composition, becomes a hit, it is a great composition. I asked him what did he mean by that, he said: 'Because any great composition speaks to the souls of a million strangers.' Two weeks later, I went out and wrote a song called *Everybody Dance*. But that's been my mission all along to try and speak to the souls of a million, or in today's world now even billions of strangers.

The positive by-product of being truthful to the deep hidden meaning, is that there's going to be fallout that touches people. They won't know why, but there is some essential truth that they're getting out of it.

I loved John-Paul Flintoff's new guide: A modest book about how to make an adequate speech. *Here's one of his insights.*

It's time to tell you about the Inuit walrus-tusk carvers.

Before the Enlightenment, most people believed that their talent was God-given. Since then, as large numbers of people have given up on God, the common view is that we ourselves are individually responsible for our creative victories – and defeats. An insight into how much more restful it must have been previously is provided by the story of Western anthropologists who visited Inuit settlements before they became westernised. The anthropologists were surprised to find that everybody they met was an artist. They all carved walrus tusks. Sometimes the carving was very good. At other times, it was so-so. But so-so carvings weren't embarrassing to the people who delivered them to the world, because they believed that "God didn't put a good carving in that tusk".

If you've been struggling to come up with an argument and a purpose for your speech or presentation, I recommend that you pretend for a moment to be an Inuit walrus-tusk carver, and hand over the responsibility to God. If you already believe that God is in charge, this will be easy. If you don't simply *pretend* that God is in charge.

Throw caution aside, and allow yourself to be boldly creative.

I find these ideas inspiring.

The main thing that I learned about conspiracy theory, is that conspiracy theorists believe in a conspiracy because that is more comforting. The truth of the world is that it is actually chaotic. The truth is that it is not The Iluminati, or The Jewish Banking Conspiracy, or the Gray Alien Theory. The truth is far more frightening. Nobody is in control. The world is rudderless.

ALAN MOORE, *THE MINDSCAPE OF ALAN MOORE*

Our culture is competent to implement almost anything and to imagine almost nothing. The same royal consciousness that makes it possible to implement anything and everything is the one that shrinks imagination because imagination is a danger. Thus every totalitarian regime is frightened of the artist. It is the vocation of the prophet to keep alive the ministry of imagination, to keep on conjuring and proposing futures alternative to the single one the king wants to urge as the only thinkable one.

WALTER BRUEGGEMANN, *THE PROPHETIC IMAGINATION*

…the ultimate, hidden truth of the world is that it is something we make and could just as easily make differently.

DAVID GRAEBER

'Everything was forever, until it was no more'

A BOOK BY ALEXEI YURCHAK

You never change things by fighting the existing reality. To change something, build a new model that makes the existing model obsolete.

BUCKMINSTER FULLER

I live in the suburbs of Bournemouth. Whenever I see another family concreting over their front garden, I'm reminded of the opening paragraph of Tolstoy's novel Resurrection.

Though men in their hundreds of thousands had tried their hardest to disfigure that little corner of the earth where they had crowded themselves together, paving the ground with stones so that nothing could grow, weeding out every blade of vegetation, filling the air with the fumes of coal and gas, cutting down the trees and driving away every beast and every bird – spring, however, was still spring, even in the town. The sun shone warm, the grass, wherever it had not been scraped away, revived and showed green not only on the narrow strips of lawn on the boulevards but between the paving-stones as well, and the birches, the poplars and the wild cherry-trees were unfolding their sticky, fragrant leaves, and the swelling buds were bursting on the lime-trees; the jackdaws, the sparrows and the pigeons were cheerfully getting their nests ready for the spring, and the flies, warmed by the sunshine, buzzed gaily along the walls. All were happy – plants, birds, insects and children. But grown-up people – adult men and women – never left off cheating and tormenting themselves with one another. It was not this spring morning which they considered sacred and important, not the beauty of God's world, given to all creatures to enjoy – a beauty which inclines the heart to peace, to harmony and to love. No, what they considered sacred and important were their own devices for wielding power over each other.

In 2008, I read a book by Nassim Nicholas Taleb called Fooled by Randomness. *I took his advice and stopped consuming news. In a Zoom discussion group this year, I was shocked by how many people are still watching. Here are his reasons:*

If an event is important enough, it will find its way to my ears.

…the accomplishment from which I derive the most pride is my weaning myself from television and the news media. I am currently so weaned that it actually costs me more energy to watch television than perform any other activity…

A journalist is trained in methods to express himself rather than to plumb the depth of things – the selection process favours the most communicative, not necessarily the most knowledgeable.

People do not realise that the media is paid to get your attention. For a journalist, silence rarely surpasses any word.

– – –

Fox News did to our parents what they thought video games would do to us.

RYAN SCOTT

Instead of consuming news, I recommend watching the very best dancers on YouTube and trying to emulate them at home (search for 'Millennium Studios'). This extract is from Keeping Together in Time, Dance and Drill in Human History *by William H. McNeill*

Human beings desperately need to belong to communities that give guidance and meaning to their lives; and moving rhythmically while giving voice together is the surest, most speedy, and efficacious way of creating and sustaining such communities that our species has ever hit upon. Words and ideals matter and are always invoked; but keeping together in time arouses warm emotions of collective solidarity and erases personal frustrations as words, by themselves, cannot do. Large and complex human societies, in all probability, cannot long maintain themselves without such kinesthetic undergirding. Ideas and ideals are not enough. Feelings matter too, and feelings are inseparable from their gestural and muscular expression.

– – –

Let us read, and let us dance; these two amusements will never do any harm to the world.

VOLTAIRE

Some comforting jokes.

To the person who stole my antidepressants. I hope you're happy.

Cicero: You need to abandon Rome immediately.

Catiline: Can we please change the subject?

Cicero: Rome needs to be immediately abandoned by you.

Q: How do you console someone with bad grammar skills?

A: There, their, they're.

Opening lines of Chairman's address at the Plastic Surgeons' Convention:

Welcome everyone, it's good to see so many new faces here today ...

Why did the French chef kill himself? He lost the *l'huile d'olive*.

Why do they put rivets in coffins? To stop oncologists prising them open and trying another dose of chemotherapy.

I told my friend, "My really annoying nephew fell into a volcano when he was on a holiday in Slovakia."

He asked, "Bratislava?"

I replied, "Well, he is now."

About ten years ago, I became very interested in the ideas behind money, and I've been reading about them ever since.

A newspaper said socialites "devote themselves to pleasure regardless of expense."

A Vanderbilt responded that actually they "devote themselves to expense regardless of pleasure."

The Western dream is to have a lot of money, and then you can lead a life of leisure and happiness. Nothing in my experience could be further from the truth.

MICHAEL PHILLIPS, *THE SEVEN LAWS OF MONEY*

Riches don't make a man richer, only busier.

Money, which represents the prose of life, and which is hardly spoken of in parlours without an apology, is in its effects and laws, as beautiful as roses.

RALPH WALDO EMERSON, *NOMINALIST AND REALIST*

TH: The tech bosses would say, "We created these fantastic tools and they're free, so what's the problem?"

JL: Well, as with lots of free things, there's more going on than one thinks. Addictive free things give over one's power to someone else and gradually degrade one's life in a horrific way. And of course they're not really free.

TOM HODGKINSON TALKS TO JARON LANIER, IDLER

This was a party game called The Perplexing Politician played by the Kensington, Chelsea, and Fulham Conservative Association in the 1920s. Each answer must be a word ending with TORY (I've updated it for the C21st).

1. A tory who makes things clear…
2. A balding tory…
3. A tory who mocks himself…
4. A tory who has fought and won…
5. A tory equipped for experiments…
6. A tory with conflicting stories…
7. A tory on the way out…
8. A volatile tory…
9. A tory in a spin…
10. A slow, tardy tory…
11. A placating tory…
12. A threatening tory…
13. A tory who praises others…
14. A grateful tory…
15. A tory who encourages stargazing…
16. A tory who makes catalogues…
17. A tory who is into compulsion…
18. A tory without a plan…
19. A tory who doesn't last…
20. A tory that collects coins…
21. A tory who provides sleeping accommodation…
22. A brusque tory…
23. A tory who spreads libel…
24. A blameless tory…
25. An eloquent tory…
26. A 'high' tory…
27. A tory who pillages…
28. A tory who delivers drugs…
29. A tory that is a large employer of labour…
30. A tory who kisses another…

1. Explanatory
2. Depilatory
3. Self-deprecatory
4. Victory
5. Laboratory
6. Contradictory
7. Valedictory
8. Inflammatory
9. Gyratory
10. Dilatory
11. Conciliatory
12. Minatory
13. Laudatory
14. Appreciatory
15. Observatory
16. Directory
17. Mandatory
18. Desultory
19. Transitory
20. Offertory
21. Dormitory
22. Peremptory
23. Defamatory
24. Exculpatory
25. Oratory
26. Hallucinatory
27. Depredatory
28. Suppository
29. Factory
30. Amatory

The HBO series Six Feet Under *shaped my attitudes to mortality. In this scene, David gets up in the early morning having been through a traumatic kidnap experience. In the hope finding some closure, David met up with his tormenter in prison. It's raining, he goes to the balcony, and talks to his dead father, Nathaniel Fisher (a regular trope in the series).*

David Fisher: I thought it would set me free, except it didn't change anything except now I know he really is insane.

Nathaniel Fisher: You're missing the point.

David Fisher: There is no point, that's the point.

[pause]

David Fisher: Isn't it?

Nathaniel Fisher: Don't give me this phoney existential bullshit, I expect better from you. The point's right in front of your face.

David Fisher: Well I'm sorry but I don't see it.

Nathaniel Fisher: You're not even grateful are ya?

David Fisher: Grateful? For the worst f**king experience of my life?

Nathaniel Fisher: You hang onto your pain like it means something, like it's worth something – well let me tell ya, it's not worth shit. Let it go. Infinite possibilities and all he can do is whine.

David Fisher: Well, what am I supposed to do?

Nathaniel Fisher: What do you think? You can do anything, you lucky bastard, you're alive!

[pause]

Nathaniel Fisher: What's a little pain compared to that?

David Fisher: It can't be so simple.

Nathaniel Fisher: What if it is?

Marie Kondo says we should only hang on to belongings which 'spark joy'. Here are three of my possessions that bring me joy.

My **Helix Metal Desktop Sharpener** (£10.55) Frustrated with perpetually breaking leads in a tiny metal sharpener, I splashed out on a deluxe model. My sons love using it, and we now have a plentiful supply of needle-sharp pencils in the house. I even spotted an arty pencil dropped on the pavement and brought it home. It sharpened up beautifully.

My **Elvis & Kresse Billfold Wallet with Coin Pocket** (£80) is made from decommissioned London Fire Brigade hose. I met Kresse over ten years ago, and I love the company story. They hit the big time when Cameron Diaz wore one of their belts on the front cover of *Vogue*. Elvis & Kresse are true alchemists turning landfill into luxury.

I'm an evangelist for the **Philips Airfryer** (£109.99). It's incredibly hard to persuade friends to change their cooking habits so I end up buying them as presents. The fryer produces crispy oven chips and my sons always get crunchy fish fingers in less than ten minutes.

We had the European Football Championships this year. Here's a best man gag for the groom who loves football…

I propose to end by comparing some golden rules for a happy marriage to something John understands…football.

1. Ensure you are fully committed every week

2. Make sure you score every Saturday

3. Don't put your tackle in too hard, or you may risk injury

4. Always make sure you change ends at half-time

5. No tackling from behind, especially on your wedding night

6. Playing away from home will result in a serious groin injury and being put on the transfer market

7. Ah there is no seven – I was going to include the one about going down in the box…but I thought better of it.

And here's a wedding anniversary joke for an Olympic year…

Theirs has been a stormy marriage, but it has been cemented by Olympic bouts of sex – that's once every four years.

Randy Olson has an intriguing theory of communication, which he aims at scientists…

When it comes to connecting with the entire audience, you have four bodily organs that are important: your head, your heart, your gut, and your sex organs. The object is to move the process down out of your head, into your heart with sincerity, into your gut with humour, and ideally, if you're sexy enough, into your lower organs with sex appeal.

A couple of Prince Philip anecdotes.

Former royal protection officer Richard Griffin has many tales of his time with Prince Philip.

When he first began working for the Duke, Mr Griffin says: "I must admit, his reputation did terrify me."

"But I quickly realised he was a very kind, considerate man."

"The wonderful story Prince Philip used to dine out on, is he rung up [my house] one day and my five-year-old son answered the phone. He [the Duke] said, "Can I speak to Dick please?"

"[My son replied] He's in the garden, I'll go and get him, who should I say is calling?" And he said, "The Duke of Edinburgh.""

"And Prince Philip said all he heard was my little boy yell out, 'Dad, can you come to the phone – someone from the pub wants to speak to you.'"

– – –

During a royal visit to a small English town, Prince Philip stopped to talk to two very old ladies. "I'm 104," boasted one of the women, "and my friend here is 101." "I don't believe it," said Philip his eyes twinkling. "Ladies always take 10 years off their age."

I discovered the concept of 'thumos' this year. American academic, Harvey Mansfield, defined 'thumos' in his Jefferson Lecture in 2007. Here are some of his key observations.

Politics is about what makes you angry, not so much about what you want. Your wants do matter, but mainly because you feel you are entitled to have them satisfied and get angry when they are not. Many times people who seem to us poor do not complain of their wants, because they do not feel entitled to those wants.

The modern philosophers behind the project of rational control were mainly afraid of *thumos* and its incitements to idealism; they laid the ground for a dull, bourgeois society lacking in both love and ambition.

Thumos shows that we are self-important animals. Having eliminated the soul, modern science cannot understand the body in its most important aspect, which is its capacity for self-importance. Modern biology, particularly the theory of evolution, is based on the overriding concern for survival in all life. This is surely wrong in regard to human life.

Thumos is not merely theoretical. To learn of it will improve your life as well as your thinking. It is up to you to improve your life by behaving as if it were important, but let me provide a summary of the things that you will know better after reflecting on the nature of *thumos*: the contrast between anger and gain; the insistence on victory; the function of protectiveness; the stubbornness of partisanship; the role of assertiveness; the ever-presence of one's own; the task of religion; the result of individuality; the ambition of greatness. Altogether *thumos* is one basis for a human science aware of the body but not bound to it, a science with soul and taught by poetry well interpreted.

One of the most electrifying moments of the year was when I was interviewing an American academic. Ten minutes before our Zoom event was about to begin, he told me he'd met Thomas Szasz. I'd never met anyone before who shared my fascination with Thomas Szasz.

Formerly, when religion was strong and science weak, men mistook magic for medicine; now, when science is strong and religion weak, men mistake medicine for magic.

Formerly, a quack was someone who had fake cures for real diseases; now he is someone who claims to have real cures for fake diseases.

Formerly, people were duped by quacks because they believed in their fake cures; now, they are duped by them because they believe in their fake diseases.

Formerly, when our religion was Christianity, we fasted and feasted; now that it is Medicine, we diet and binge. Thus was gluttony replaced by obesity, prayer by psychotherapy, the monastery by the health spa, the clergyman by the clinician, the Vatican by the Food and Drug Administration, and God for whom being slim meant being virtuous by Medical Science for which it means being healthy.

THE UNTAMED TONGUE, A DISSENTING DICTIONARY

Some quirky insights.

The more a thing tends to be permanent, the more it tends to be lifeless.

ALAN WATTS

Reality, is that which, when you stop believing in it, doesn't go away.

PHILIP K. DICK

Tell all the truth, but tell it slant. Success in circuit lies.

EMILY DICKINSON

In a 2014 World Bank report, it was found that out of about 1500 reports produced in the years 2008 to 2012, 517 of them were never downloaded at all.

In academia, the standard measure for plagiarism is "eight words in the same sequence."

Nothing risqué, nothing gained.

ALEXANDER WOOLLCOTT

John D Rockefeller's favourite poem

A wise old owl lived in an oak
The more he saw the less he spoke,
The less he spoke, the more he heard,
Why aren't we all like that wise old bird?

Theodore Zeldin is another Oxonian. He wrote a book called The Hidden Pleasures of Life, *which contains these ideas.*

The fatal disease that attacks the living is *rigor vitae*, rigidity of the mind, which burns up curiosity and replaces it with repetitive and numb routine; it is more dangerous than *rigor mortis* because it gives the illusion of being alive. One is only nominally alive if one is incapable of giving birth to thoughts one has never had before and of being inspired by what others think.

Those who have power or money have their own idea about how to make everyone happy which is by giving everyone more power and money.

Kind people commit suicide when they enter professions where there is no room for kindness. The most frequent form of suicide is to lose hope.

It is above all through private conversations that people obtain the reassurance and courage to attempt what they may have never thought possible before, find partners enabling them to do something they could not have done alone, and become animated with the feeling that by discovering others and being discovered by others, and by assimilating what each gives the other, they have become more fully alive. Appreciation, affection and animation are what private life can add to public life.

I love Geoff Burch's business books. He frequently refers to this emblem featuring two vultures sitting on a branch, which he had printed on a T-shirt. The moral is if you know what you want for your business, you've got to go out and get it. As Jack London put it: 'You can't wait for inspiration. You've got to go after it with a club.'

My other favourite mantra from Geoff Burch comes from his anecdote about visiting a pig farmer who lovingly coddled his pigs. Geoff was horrified when the farmer pointed to Rosie and said she was going off to become bacon within a week. The farmer countered that well-treated pigs produce fine meat, battery-bred, stressed pigs do not. The business lesson: *Don't delight your customers, make bacon out of them.*

I found a book of the favourite prayers of famous people in a chapel while I was on holiday. The former Archbishop of Canterbury, Robert Runcie, chose St Teresa's Bookmark. He had it printed at the beginning of his Prayer Book and commented, 'it is something that has steadied me and strengthened me in times of trial and moments of doubt.'

Let nothing disturb thee,
Nothing affright thee;
All things are passing:
God never changeth:
Patient endurance
Attaineth to all things
Who God possesseth
In nothing is wanting.
Alone God sufficeth.

Lord Runcie also submitted a prayer which was pinned above the desk of a holy nun, a friend of his. It simply said,

God bless this mess.

Uplifting thoughts for 2022.

For reasons I have never understood, people like to hear that the world is going to hell.

DEIDRE MCCLOSKEY

Adversity is good for you. It prepares you for more adversity.

CHARLIE BROWN

The point of getting out of bed in the morning is to bring about the future. And that's why I loathe nostalgia.

ALAN GARNER

Enver Hoxha's upbeat New Year Message of 1967 to the Albanian people: "This year will be harder than last year. However, it will be easier than next year."

The past is terrible, the present is catastrophic, thank goodness we don't have a future!

ARMENIAN PROVERB

We physicists believe the separation between past, present and future is only an illusion, although a convincing one.

ALBERT EINSTEIN

Immensis laboribus comparatur eruditio: ac post moriendum est.
With immense labour learning is obtained: and then you have to die.

What a wonderful life I've had! I only wish I'd realised it sooner.

LETTE